"Get Out Of Debt"
(c) copyright Peter LeGrove 2021
All Rights Reserved
This book or any portion thereof
may not be reproduced or used in any manner whatsoever
without the express written permission of the publisher
except for the use of brief quotations in a book review.

plegrove@gmail.com

www.animalsdinosaursandbugs.com

Live Cheap In An UnCheap World

Disclaimer

Although the author and publisher have made every effort to ensure that the information in this book was correct at press time, the author and publisher do not assume and hereby disclaim any liability to any party for any loss, damage, or disruption caused by errors or omissions, whether such errors or omissions result from negligence, accident, or any other cause.

This book is for entertainment purposes only. The views expressed are of the author alone and should not be taken as expert advice. The reader is responsible for his own actions. Neither the author or the publisher assume any liability or responsibility on behalf of the reader or purchaser of this material.

Who Will Benefit From This Book

This little book is for anyone who is struggling to get out of debt or just make ends meet. And for the few who want to start saving again. Life is difficult out there and changing one's spending habits is a start. There are some little things you can do to help you not spend so much. Cutting out the good things in life is not easy, especially if you have kids.

This book is not for the instant generation, as most new things you have to learn. And learning takes time. This book tries to shorten the learning curve, by showing you how to get up to speed on a new subject, quickly and cheaply. If you are into checking out what you can do online and getting up to speed in your chosen field, then this book is for you.

The people on the planet, at the moment, are in the cusp of change and this book will help you stay ahead of the game. With the internet and the wired world, there are many new opportunities available out there in cyberspace. But you need to know what they are, and this book makes a few more opportunities available to you. All you have to do is grab them.

How To Use This Book

This book is about ideas, so read through the book to find out what you could use in your situation. And keep your eyes open to new ideas. Like people who smoke and complain about the price of cigarettes. Why not grow your own tobacco?
There are things you can do starting now, that could make a difference in you life rather fast. But most things take time. There is a learning curve. Even with growing vegetables, your first attempt will not be very good. But then again, vegetables you get from the supermarket are a lot better looking than what you can grow yourself. So you have to get used to a different standard of quality.
There are ideas scattered throughout the book of what real people are doing now. You could call them case studies. If someone else is doing it, then you can do it too. Check out the freelancer sites, join a few and quote for some jobs, and see what happens.

What Is In This Book

Introduction
Buying A House Time
Buying A Car
Finding Cheap Rent
Now Credit Cards
How To Get Out Of Debt
What Happened To Me
What Is Happening Now
Budgeting, Saving And Planning
What To Do With Cars
New Technology
What You Can Do
Starting On The Internet
Bricks And Mortar Businesses
Teach English Online
Set Yourself Up As A FreeLancer
Selling Stuff
Grow Your Own Vegetables
Take Advantage Of High Prices
Ask Around Generation
Shopping
The Ultimate Live Cheap
The Last Word

Your Free Book

As a way of saying thank you for buying my book I'm offering you a free book.

This book "How To Add Qualifications To Your CV Using FREE Courses" is about what you can learn over the internet for free. It shows you where to go to get Certificates of Accomplishment that you can add to your CV.

Click here and you will be taken to another page where you can download the free book.

Get Your FREE book here
http://animalsdinosaursandbugs.com/MOOC-download.html

Introduction

Debt is a part of our life now, so give up "Keeping Up With The Jones" because that mentality is just going to keep you in debt. Debt has slowly crept into our lives and it has got to the point where it controls what we do. And sometimes we suddenly find that it controls us. Before debt was usually manageable but as expenses have increased and pay-checks haven't, debt can sometimes seem like a big heavy block holding us back. As taxes and secondary tax are taking more away and giving less back, problems are starting to arise. Also every new regulation introduced by our unelected and elected officials just so they can keep their jobs puts the price up. And that includes added expenses like fixing your car and doing home repairs, as well as everything you buy. Now we live in an over regulated society where our quality of life has decreased as our debt levels have increased. So the new regulations have increased our cost of living but done very little for our safety and happiness.

At the moment the most expensive expenses are rent and gas for your car as well as electricity, internet and food. So at the end of the week you have nothing left so it is time to bring out the credit card and that is fatal. The bottomless pit just got deeper.

Buying A House Time

Now this might sound really dumb but the easiest way to control debt is not to take on too much debt at the beginning. And that is very difficult because the bank says you can get this much for a mortgage and our mentality is to try and get the largest mortgage you are allowed. 'Change Your Way Of Thinking.' And some banks are not very happy when you want less, so stay away from bank managers if you can. It has got to the point now where I believe nothing I hear in a bank. At one bank when I was looking to buy a home to live in, the bank said I had to put everything in their bank. That meant all money coming in, all money going out and my meagre savings. I said "I'm not doing that." And walked out. Now at another bank when I wanted to buy a home in a small town near the big city and commute to work, they said the mortgage was too little and head office had to approve it. That is how stupid the debt situation has become, I could get a $220,000 mortgage approved by the bank in the small town where most houses were selling for way under $200,000 but if I wanted a mortgage for a house under $100,000 I had to get approved by head office. How stupid. Now for the real stupid, I had trouble believing this. I wanted to buy a lifestyle block way out in the country with a church on it. It was only a little block probably around 5 acres and the bank said I had to put it in dairy farming if I wanted a mortgage. I couldn't believe what I was hearing so I gave up on that idea.

Now with the price of houses way out of reach of the common family the best you can do is buy a dump in a good part of town and do it up. But even now most of the dump houses have been sold. When house prices start going up the dump houses end up on the market and now I think most dump house have been sold, renovated and resold. So finding a cheap place to buy is getting more and more difficult. But not to worry there will be an economic reset pretty soon and house prices will come down again.

NOW before you do anything read about what you need to know. In this book you will learn where to find cheap information and I would advise learning as much as you need to know about buying your home and this way banks will have more than a few problems taking advantage of you.

At the moment if you already have a mortgage and are having problems with debt start selling off your excess stuff on your local auction site. Just to de-clutter and to give you an idea of the prices available when you want to buy more stuff again. And if the house prices in your country are very high think about selling. Now don't do what everybody else does and that is buy another house. I would go back to renting and leave what money you have left over after paying off your mortgage, in the bank until the house prices drop substantially. And they will, they always do and bank managers and real estate agents will say they don't. I had a real estate agent tell me that selling your house to go back renting was not a good idea as rents were very high and a lot of rental properties were going off the market. What she said was true but your endgame is to buy a house after the prices come down. That is why you need to de-clutter so you have less material things to carry around. We moved four times in six years. You have to follow the market and see for yourself. Look what happened after 2008. 'House Prices Do Not Always Keep Going Up', just remember that and you want to get in near the bottom. Then if you have cash you can use a Cash Offer to get a better price. 'Cash Is King' remember that. To get out of debt do not do what everybody else is doing as their mentality is different from yours.

Do Not Buy A House You Cannot Afford. There is a very big difference between what the bank says you can afford and what you can afford so don't listen to the bank. Buy the cheapest house you can find in a reasonable part of town and live there. It might not be as good as living in the best part of town and the schools will not be as good and the crime rate will be worse, but then again your debt levels will not be too high.

Buying A Car

Forget the garbage about buying the most expensive car you think you can afford. A car gets you from A to B and hopefully back again. So you don't need a second mortgage to buy a car. The price of second hand cars is coming down and it seem to be dropping quite rapidly. When buying a second hand car try and find a backyard mechanic who can fix it on the cheap. There are many backyard mechanics and very cheap licensed garages who will fix your car for a reasonable price. As an example my sister's car which they brought very cheap about 12 years ago had a serious problem. So they got a quote from the garages near where they live and the cheapest from the guy from India was around $700 and the most expensive price at another garage was over $3000. So it pays to shop around and my sister's car is still going.

I brought a car from a car fair for $1500 and seven years later it is still going. Other than maintenance the only problem was a seat belt. And I have a back yard mechanic that keeps it going. So forget expensive. I have two cheap cars so if one breaks down I can use the other one. And for the price of two cheap cars I doubt if I could have got a good car for the amount of money I spent on two cars. To buy anything on the cheap you must ask around. There is a chapter on asking around later in this book.

Finding Cheap Rent

Now this is difficult, other than joining a tent city you could have problems. One way is trading your labour for rent. In a backpacker hostel or any hostel for that matter you can work for a room. You usually end up cleaning the hostel but it is free rent. You can usually find jobs like this on the backpacker boards on the internet. You can do the same in camp grounds but you or your wife will have to be there, you cannot leave the place empty. Now we are back to ask around. Just remember it is written in the Bible "Ask and you shall receive" so start asking. My friend lived in the countryside and worked in the city and the price of petrol went up he started looking for somewhere to stay in the city. Now he nearly ended up in a hostel looking after the boarders but he turned that down for a room in an unregistered hostel that was cheap, but you had to put up with a lot of poverty and addiction issues with the other people living there. If you have a family it will be more difficult.

Now Credit Cards

Credit cards come under the beautiful but deadly category. I learned very young how dangerous they were and didn't have one for many years but now with internet shopping I need one. But I only use it on the internet and I pay it off as soon as I use it. And I only have one credit card. I don't like to say this but you do need a credit card. They do make life easier but you should only use it when there is no other option. I never use it to go into debt as that is the most expensive debt you can get. And when you cancel your credit card you end up paying a big closing account fee, so be careful, banks love their fees. If you end up in the situation where your credit card is maxed out, go to another bank and get a loan to pay it off as bank interest rates should be cheaper but now they seem to be catching up with credit card interest rates. Then live without a credit card and that could be the most difficult time of your life.

How To Get Out Of Debt

"Live Within Your Means Do Not Try To Keep Up With The Jones" Tell your family what is happening and all pull together to change it. Why do it all alone. Also I am a firm believer in Temp Agencies. They are amazing and as long as you can pass a drug test, get to work on time and do some work while you are there, you'll always have a job. I do recommend you join more than one agency to see who can get you a good job. I ended up working full time in one factory, an excellent job. Then I went to another city and the agency got me another good job at a factory in that city. So as long as you have good work ethics you will always have a job. Admittedly you won't make a fortune but you will make some money and it all helps.

Also to get out of debt you have to swallow your pride. Me and my wife go to free church dinners, shop at opportunity shops, get free bread at the charity food bank. Before I used to hope nobody would see us but now I don't worry. We don't break the law, we don't steal and we follow the law when we drive. Living cheap doesn't mean we are destitute but sometimes we are pretty close.

When getting out of debt there are only a few things you have to do. The first one is DO NOT take on any new debt, so that means you have to live within your means. In other words you need to change your shopping habits. We do not have set items to buy, we only buy what is on special and what has been marked down. That means we only buy meat that has been reduced as it has been sitting in the chiller too long. I try and buy meat that has been reduced twice that way it is closer to half price. We usually get bread free from the charity shop as the supermarket has donated it to be given away. And we get vegetables from the weekend markets where they are cheaper and you can bargain. Anything else we buy we always ask ourselves "Do we need this?" and if we don't we don't buy it. Buying gas for the car is something we need so now we just don't drive as much. Now the other thing you need to do is Make More Money and there are chapters in this book that show you how to do just that, you just have to try out and find what is a good fit for you.

Now the easiest way to get out of debt is don't get into it, but in today's world that is nearly impossible. So the next best thing is don't get into unnecessary debt. Still very difficult in a consumer society. Now if you find yourself so overwhelmed with debt it is time to do something about it. Get a second job, work yourself to death and or do things you will find out in this book. But use the extra cash to pay off debt not buy new stuff or live extravagantly. Even before you start to make more money start paying off debt. We used to do 'debt consolidation' where you get a personal loan from your main bank to pay off your credit card and other high interest debt. Except nowadays personal loans are not cheap anymore. So to get your debt under control find a piece of paper and write down by hand all your debts and the minimum payment each month, and stick it on your computer screen and the fridge. Start with the smallest debt at the top of the page going down the page to the largest which should be your mortgage. Alternatively you could write down the most expensive debt, the one with the highest interest rate at the top and work down to the cheapest. You will see the most expensive debt is credit card debt. Don't tackle your mortgage just yet as that should be the lowest interest rate.

The idea is to pay off the minimum amount each month so you do not get any extra fees added on. And pay any extra money into paying off the smallest debt or the highest interest rate debt. Then when you have paid that debt off, start paying off the next lowest debt on the list and so on and so on. Put a big line through the debt that has been paid off and write paid beside it. This way if it is on the fridge you and your family can see that one debt is paid off so the system is working. Then cut up the store credit card and burn it. All I have in my wallet now are discount club cards, no store credit cards. And doing this over time you will get rid of your debt.

That is the general idea of getting out of debt and now the other side of the equation is making more money and not spending it on silly things, usually called 'dumb money'. That is do not buy things you do not need or do not buy something very expensive when a cheaper version will do just as well, for example cars. If you have expensive habits try and stop them. Your world will not end if you stop going to the bar, you could go one night a week instead of three or four nights. Buy a cook book and stop eating out. Rearrange your life so you do not spend so much money. Don't do it suddenly just bring it on slowly or your family will not be very happy. And or you could try and switch off ever screen in your house and have a talk. Tell your family the situation and tell them what is going to happen. You could also play a game where you see who does not spend the most money. You need to get your family on board, everybody working together. This book goes into how not to spend so much money.

There is a lot of talk about budgeting but I don't do too much budgeting. It is quite simple when your goal is to be debt free all money goes to pay down one debt at a time. With budgeting I just like to know where the money goes so I always collect receipts and add them up at the end of the month and what is left pays off debt. I always keep a bit of cash in the bank just in case something crops up like a car repair. You should be driving more carefully and parking properly so you should not get any traffic tickets. And all your licenses and taxes should be paid for and up to date. Insurance is another major expense and I do keep adjusting my insurance down so it is more affordable. Now with the internet that is very easy to do. If I need something expensive I start saving, no more going into debt.

Anyway the following chapters are about how we lived cheap so we could get out of debt

What Happened To Me
I thought everything was okay, but it wasn't. The company I worked for didn't recover from the 2008 financial crisis and shut down. So I was out of a job. I didn't have a lot of money in the bank to fall back on. So I had to do some serious rearranging with my life and the situation I was in. Jobs were very hard to find, ever labouring jobs. So to try and keep on top of what was going on, I started selling everything I didn't need in the weekend markets. That was not very profitable. I picked up odd jobs here and there but nothing continuous. Living in the city was expensive, so I headed out of the city into a small country town where rents were a lot cheaper. Here permanent jobs were nearly non existent so I lived off part time work on the farms. And that keep me going and brought in a bit of extra cash.

Here I could start a garden, before in the apartment I couldn't do that. I had been playing around on the internet for a while, so I kept doing that and that helped. I was still doing the markets but that was more of a hobby thing. I knew all the cheap and free places to eat. I collected driftwood for firewood and there was a saving there. I cut back on buying things and if I needed anything I would shop at the charity shops and go to rummage sales. I brought a small car that didn't use much gas and there was a big saving there. But most important I started meeting people and building my network. I was doing volunteer work at the local radio station and the country garden and I started to fit in. Somewhere between then and now I had maxed out my credit cards and now it was time to do something about getting my life back in order.

This book is about what I did to reinvent myself so I could "Get Out Of Debt." I did it, not because I wanted to but because I had too. Without a steady income life can be difficult. I have to thank the tax payer and the government for the social welfare programs that are available. Without which I would have been in dire straights.

What Is Happening Now
Right now in 2020 the world has gone mad, it has changed completely from what it was like when I was young. The government has gone tax mad and regulation mad. And to top it off we have the added expense of the internet. Electricity prices keep going up, and rents are definitely not cheap anymore. And if you have made the biggest investment of your life and actually brought your house, you can guarantee land taxes will go up and keep going up. And while keeping up with world events, the price of oil has increased so the price of gas at the pump has also increased. You would think the government would use some tax relief on gas but that would give them less money to waste. We are getting screwed on all sides. What about milk - the bottom has fallen out of the world price, but on the supermarket shelf the price hasn't moved.

All expenses have gone up, but wages and if you are on the pension, nothing has moved up. Things are not good on the home front. Getting out of debt is something your parents used to do, and something you'd love to do, but there is nothing left at the end of the week. Money just slips through your fingers. Even now if you have a job, you still need to have a plan to save money.

If you are living paycheck to paycheck, you cannot afford any hiccups. Even the price of food has gone through the roof. Bread a staple food, and butter, has gone out of reach of anybody pinching pennies. Just to survive you need to keep track of how much money slips through your fingers.

The worst expense is the rent, and that comes out every week. That is first expense and there is not much left after that. Now, how do you pay cheap rent? I know one guy who lives in a van. All he pays is the parking space in a covered, locked, parking garage. And that is a lot cheaper than paying rent on a room or apartment. It takes a while to get to know what any place has to offer, so you got to ask around. In the end he knew all the toilets, where to go for a shower, cost $2 and all the churches and community places that handed out free food. He lived very cheap and loved it. The garage he lived in was pretty run down, had spaces for about 30 cars, but after work and on the weekends he had the whole place to himself. But not everybody can do that. What if you've got a family? He was on his own.

Also every month expenses like water and electricity has just increased incredibly. And the new expense, the internet has added a new monthly bill that has to be paid. About 10 years ago that was not an every month expense. We could call it a modern expense. But with the internet we don't need TV and the cable companies. We can also forget about the everyday newspapers and even books for that matter. So there is a few savings there.

Everybody talks about budgeting, but all I do is try and keep track of where it all goes. I keep receipts from everything and add them up at the end of the month. That is on top of all the other expenses, like the car. That is a major expense added onto all the other monthly expenses. If you know where the money goes you can plug the leaks, so the first thing to do is to keep all receipts, and know where it is going out. Very difficult to budget when you are living money in money out. Then there are the yearly expenses like taxes that sneak up on you and they aren't cheap. How can you budget when you have nothing to budget with?

Another major expense is health, especially dentists. Now with dentists it does pay to shop around and ask around, because believe it or not there are cheap dentists out there. I used to go to one run by a church organization. I had to pay but it was very cheap. I have heard some incredible cheap prices for dental work, as well as some amazingly expensive prices for the same thing, so look around. At the local university you could book in, so the students learning dentistry could practice on your teeth. They were good as they were supervised. You weren't putting your teeth in anybody's hands. When you are living cheap looking after your teeth is a plus. When I get a toothache, I mix up baking soda and hydrogen peroxide and that usually keeps it under control. I also floss as that helps.

One of the easiest things to change and the most difficult to follow through on is – changing your buying habits. Now for this you cannot go cold turkey. Your kids and your wife or husband will not let you. So you have to bring it in slowly. To start, if you are walking past a second hand shop and or a church charity shop, walk in and have a look. Now some of these places are not all that cheap, so know the prices at the department stores. Nowadays with all the specials on in the shops it can be cheaper to buy what you want on special. Stop impulse buying. Plan what you want to buy. And always ask yourself "Do we really need this?" If you do, keep looking for it on special or second hand.

Budgeting, Saving And Planning

To survive to get out of debt you must know how much money is coming in, and how much is going out. Hopefully more is coming in than going out and you can save the difference. You do need some money in the bank for little things that sneak up on you, like car repairs and taxes. And I think the main goal of getting out of debt is to save some money. But in today's world you have to live cheap just to survive.

You should try to avoid fees, especially bank fees. I didn't realize it but my bank account had an overdraft limit. When I went into overdraft I didn't even know until I checked the account. The bank didn't send me an email or nothing, and I was overdrawn for a while. Then I got lumbered with a fee, so I marched into the bank and asked them to remove the overdraft. That is a thing they call an automatic overdraft to help you out of course, but also to boost their bottom line. I prefer cash to money in the bank. Another thing is credit cards. They are dangerous but necessary. I learnt very young just how dangerous they were. In the end I had to cut my credit cards up and close the account. Then I got lumbered with a close account fee which was not cheap. So now I only have one credit card which I use in times of emergency.

I use the simplest of budgets, Keep all receipts food, gas and what ever in a bag and then add them up at the end of the month. So I know how much is going out. I don't do very much impulse buying except at garage sales, and when I get home after garage sales I write down everything I brought. There are a few places that still take cash and I try to keep track of all cash going out.

On the other side of the ledger I keep track of everything that comes in. Most goes direct into the bank but things like selling on facebook are still cash. I do try to save mainly for things that creep up on you. Like the car breaking down and taxes, house and car. The taxes on the house run about $3000 and the car goes over $300 a year and I've got 2 cars, so I've got to save enough to keep the tax man happy.

I must live an incredibly boring life, I probably go out for one coffee a month and sometimes fast food when I am hungry, and that is about it. Never go to the pub, just drink my homebrew wine and that keeps me going. My cheap treat is chocolate but I only buy when on special.

What To Do With Cars

Cars are expensive and getting them fixed is even more expensive. I only buy cars around 15 to 20 years old. I keep looking until the car I want comes along at the right price. If it is a small engine car I'm after, I just look at small engine cars. I try to never be in a situation where I have to buy. When I was sick of paying a $100 dollars to full up the car, I started looking at small engine cars with low mileage around 5 years old. I didn't know anything about small cars then, but now I know a lot. I lived on the internet and had alerts in my area for small cars. Then one came along. It had under a 100,000 on the clock and all the paper work was up to scratch. It just needed new tires and was around $3,000. We went to the bank and they wouldn't give me a loan, so I brought it on my credit card. Then I went back to the same back and asked them if I could get a loan to pay off my credit card. And they said "Yes" so I paid off the high interest credit card with a normal interest bank loan. Doing this gave me my credit card credit to fall back on.

This car costs just over $50 to fill up and goes further than the big car. I asked my back yard mechanic about tires and he said "No problem." He then went to the car wreckers and picked up 4 nearly brand new tires for about a third of the price to buy brand new. Then off to a fix it garage to get the tires put on. It didn't end there. About a month later the car needed a new battery, so off he went to the wreckers again, and picked up a near new battery for under half the new price. And so far that is about all the car has needed.

It is very handy to know a back yard mechanic, as they can save you a fortune. I buy the oil and the oil filter and he changes the oil for $30. Also when you need to get your car fixed and the back yard mechanic can't do it, it pays to shop around. My sister had a serious problem with her car and she got three quotes, ranging from $3.000 to $700. Now we have a real mechanic we can go to. Even my mechanic was surprised when she got it fixed for that price. And he didn't add anything onto the price. To find out who is a back yard mechanic, just ask around, someone will know somebody. That is the way now, just ask and you shall receive. I would say having the backyard mechanic has saved a lot of money and usually car bills are not cheap. So I would recommend getting to know one, and also having a network of friends who can do things.

People are very versatile, and there are people out there that will love to help for a bit of cash. It all boils down to asking around. I still have the big car and if anyone wants to borrow it, they just got to put some gas in it and they can have it. That has helped a lot of people and I can call on them if I need a hand. Networking doesn't just work for business. I have also surrounded myself with retired advisers, mainly to do with fixing the house. They tell me what products to buy, and what to do and how to do it. To keep things cheap you need a Do It Yourself mentality.

Also I shop around for gas or petrol as the price varies quite a lot from gas station to gas station. Now I have a fair idea who has the cheapest gas in my area, so I only buy gas there. And driving habits make a big difference. I don't drive hard or fast and I keep my foot off the metal. My sister was driving my car and I'm sure she drove about 100kms less than I do on a tank of gas. I was amazed at how far the car didn't go when she was driving. That was in the big car. She could only drive the automatic, not the manual car. So keep your foot off the floor and you will go a lot further on a tank. And at over $100 to fill her up you will go further.

New Technology

I have really embraced the new technology generation, and if I need to know something the first thing I do is "Google it." Then I know what I am talking about when I talk to my advisers, and they are the people with boots on the ground experience. I usually do what they say, so I can keep them on my side.

The internet is an amazing tool, instant information at your fingertips. But you can very easily get caught up with information overload. To actually get a grip on information overload I found it took a bit of time. First I had to surround myself with websites that had what I was looking for. And it does take a while to sift the wheat from the chaff. Then all you have to do is upgrade your reference sites. Now I am pretty set, I have my sites for gardening and fixing the house, and whatever else I need.

If I am looking up a new topic, and I need to get a list of knowledgeable sites, I first type in the keyword. That is very important getting the keywords correct. If you do not get what you are after, change the keywords. This should bring up a whole new set of articles. Perfecting search will save you time. And after you have your own list of sites you like, then that is all you need until a new site comes along.

One site I keep a close eye on is http://www.giveawayofthe day.com, because everyday they have a free give away, and some are very good. I have joined their mailing list so I get an email everyday. And I usually check them out. First I read the comments then I know if the program is any good. And some programs are exceptional. After reading a few of the comments you will soon know if the give away is any good or not. So if you are living cheap, this is a site to keep an eye on as they have some very good stuff. But the give away of the day is only FREE for 24 hours, then they bring out a new give away. So get it while it is hot.

Living cheap doesn't mean you have to be cheap. Amazon.com is the place to go for books and TV. I don't have a TV I just use amazon prime for and that gives me everything I need or want. To find out anything just go to amazon kindle and you have a library at your finger tips of everything you want to find out. Amazon prime is read for free, but if you don't want amazon prime just go to free ebooks on kindle and download what you want to read. The free ebooks are usually free for a day or two with the maximum up to five days, so load up your kindle. Download the FREE kindle reader from amazon.com, and then you can read the books on your phone, on your tablet or computer or whatever. To find the free books can be a bit of a mission. Amazon doesn't want to give them away. Just search for 'Top 100 free kindle books' on amazon and that is where they are. I sometimes click the lowest price and that brings up the books for $0. Kindle is a lot of fun. Learning curve seems a bit steep, but it is well worth figuring it out. Now with kindle you can learn everything you want, cheaper. Technology is amazing. And if you want to buy a book they are cheap, mostly under $4.

For the latest hot fiction just go to your local library, but for information there is not much that will beat kindle. You can learn whatever you want for a very small fee. But then sometimes you can buy a book that is not really what you thought it was. I've had highly recommended books that were not for me. So now if I am really serious about learning something, I will usually find a blog that I like then I will buy the book that the author of the blog has written. I try to keep away from impulse buying. That is usually when I usually buy something that is not really what I want.

Even for seminar stuff, if you are into seminars, you can usually pick up the ebook the seminar comes from, for around on average under $4. Also before most pdf information products were priced somewhere between $20 and $30 for around a 50 page pdf ebook. Now you should be able to pick up the same information on kindle for under $4. The cost of learning a new skill has just come way down. The same is now starting to apply to courses on Udemy and these prices have come way down now. If you see a course you would like to learn, check out kindle and see if the book is available. And for around $4 you will get the same information, instead of buying the course. With online information there seems to be a stepping stone, depending on how much you want to pay. The cheapest is kindle, at around $3. Then onto the online course that usually goes for around $300. And at the very top of the information scale, is the in person seminar going for around $5000. And basically the information is the same, the difference is the way you receive it. We are into cheap so we stick to kindle.

Talking about free courses over the internet, try out MOOCs, Massive Open Online Course, and see what you would like to learn. I used to say I was a MMOGer now I am a MOOCer. They are very addictive, and it is amazing what you will learn and the friends you will meet on the forums. And in a lot of cases you will receive a "Certificate of Accomplishment". That is the future of education. I do MOOCs across all platforms. Like Coursera, Canvas.net, NovoEd, Udacity, edX, FutureLearn and Open2Study to name a few. There are heaps of MOOCs to choose from. I like the real time MOOCs as opposed to the 'do when you feel like it' MOOC. Real time MOOCs give you deadlines so your assignments have to be in, and all the quizzes completed each week before the deadline. But the deadlines are pretty flexible, except the final deadline. And if you are going for a certificate you need to keep within the deadlines or you will miss out. Now I only do MOOCs that give a certificate. Need something to show for my effort.

What You Can Do

Now kindle and MOOCs are where you get the information, and here is where you use it to make money. There are a number of freelancer or micro job sites, like Fiverr and Upwork. These two have been around longer than most, but they are not the only ones. There are many freelancer sites like Guru, Microworkers, SEOclerks, and Freelancer. Check them out and see what you think. I would apply for more than one as there is a lot of competition out there. Take your pick they all do the same thing. You have to find a site where you can sell your skill set. I think the most profitable marketable skill is something that helps other people make money. At the moment the hottest thing in cyberspace is Facebook advertisements, soon to be overtaken by Linkedin advertisements. These are pay per click similar to google adwords but they are new. Linkedin adwords is so new very few people know how to do it. So if you have mastered Linkedin adwords you can write your own ticket. But you must be able to produce results. If you don't or can't you will be pushed aside by someone who can and if you are helping people make money, you should get a better hourly rate.

Now when you are dealing worldwide on a 24 hour basis, the world's cheapest salary is the bottom rate. And you will find some payments quoted are ridiculous but someone in Asia or the old Eastern Bloc will think they are the best salary ever. So some things you can forget about like writing articles or ebooks or ghost writing. At $1 a 100 words and up to $3 a 100, you have to be either desperate, or living in some back water village in Vietnam or Croatia or some place like that. Unless you can type one hundred words per minute and then you still have to research the topic. But then again, if you can put together a sales page that makes money, your payment goes way up. The specialist skills are what brings in the money. So before you spend hours learning a new skill and setting yourself up, make sure the skill is in demand and the salary range is worth it. I first heard this from Dan Kennedy from Magnetic Marketing fame, whether he was the first to say it or not, I don't know. "It took me five years to become an overnight success." And that is not far wrong. As you will find out very soon, when you start marketing yourself on freelancer sites or blog sites or where ever you choose to make some extra money.

If you want to try freelancing then read everything on the sites, especially the free pdf download about how to set up to get seen. As that is a big problem, getting noticed and then apply for everything you can that is listed on your profile. And just get something to put on your profile. Check out kindle and see if they have a cheap book on freelancing just to get you started. To survive living cheap you have to learn new skills, and the sooner you learn the new skill, the sooner you can start using it. And it is always better to learn from somebody who has mastered the skill, than trial and error which is a very slow way of doing things.

One of the biggest rages at the moment is self publishing on kindle. But just remember, it takes five years to become an overnight success. So the more learning you do from the masters, the shorter the five years gets. And to survive you have to shorten the five years. That is where kindle comes in. Read everything you can on what you are learning. The sooner you master it, the sooner you will profit from what you have learned. Publishing on kindle is a lot of learning, but be thankful many authors have already done it and written about it. So read up on what they did and do it. I don't know how long kindle will be the rage, and publishing on kindle is very easy. But making money from selling books is not. So if you want to go that route, start reading and doing.

Always follow the money. And to learn a new topic is getting cheaper with kindle. You can read three to six books, and you will be very clued up on a new idea to make money, for less than $30. Then again the people who read the most books and are good at teaching, make the most money. Tony Robbins has read nearly every book on personal development, and tried out what they said and now look at him. The key is reading the book then doing what the book suggests. The more times you do this, the more you will learn and know what works and what doesn't.

Starting On The Internet

If you are planning anything along the lines of an internet business, start getting an email list together because you are going to need it. The gurus say the money is in the list, so the sooner you start the list the sooner you get ahead. Take advantage of other people's knowledge, and you will reach your goal a lot sooner. Why reinvent the wheel, when you can copy what other people have already done. That will get you where you are going a lot sooner.

There are a lot of different ideas on the internet about what you can do for an internet business. If any of these ideas resonate with you, check them out to find out the cost of entry. That means starting at the cheapest, which is kindle, and reading a few books about what you have to do to succeed in the brave new world of the internet. If you watch the online free seminar for the online course just remember the golden rule, "It took me five years to become an overnight success." I would say most of the people who make a success overnight have spent the past five years building up their email list, their facebook fan page, their linkedin profile and their websites, so they already know a bit about what to do on the internet. So if it takes you a bit longer don't worry too much you'll get there. Here, if you are going to pick a new idea, pick something in a small niche and hope it is not over crowded. If you pick a niche that anybody can do, there is a lot of competition and that lowers the price. Just for an example, I was watching a seminar for a type of video advertisement and it looked very promising. If I was into video and the technical stuff I needed to know to get it off the ground, I would seriously consider something like that. It was a small niche therefore not too overcrowded, and the end product did sell itself. All you had to do was get customers and that is the most difficult part.

This comes under helping people make more money. And that is the best side of the coin to be on. If you help a business owner, or anybody for that matter, make money or save money, you are in demand. It is just like my backyard mechanic. He saved me a lot of money buying used parts, so if I have any problems with my car I know where I am going to go. He has a customer for life, and a customer for life is what you are after.

Now back to the video advertisement. Making the video is the easy part, but to get a customer for life you have to get someone to buy off the video. Now that is the difficult part. So to set yourself up in the internet world, you need to go the extra mile. That is, make the video and set it up so it is found and people buy off it. We are into life long learning now, so don't ever think you can learn one thing and that will set you up for life. The ultimate goal is to help people make more money.

Another niche I dabble in is setting small businesses up with a website. My web design skills are something to be desired, but my marketing skills to drive people to the website are not. I just play by the book, and do what the gurus say and it works. So the website doesn't really matter, it is the end product which is new customers that matters. I even set up free websites and as long as they get customers, that is all that matters. So always think, how can I help you make more money or save money. The internet is only one tool, mind you it is a very new tool, but the learning curve can be quite daunting with many roller coaster rides. And also the half life of most stuff on the internet is not very long. There is always something new that is the rage, and in a few months it will all be forgotten. The idea is to pick something that will last more than a few months. Hopefully it is something you can repackage, or combine with the next latest rage so you can keep it going. The bottom line is to learn something that will help customers make more money or save money.

Before you start on the internet look at some of the free seminars and decide which one you like. Then check out kindle to see what is available. Usually a few months or weeks after the seminar, somebody who brought the seminar, will bring out the kindle book for next to nothing. A lot of seminars are very expensive and that is a large investment you have to make. I was looking at free seminars about facebook ads. The first one I watched I did everything he said in the free seminar and I still couldn't make it work. So I looked at another seminar and this one looked promising. I checked out his blog and joined the website and started reading his material, but I still couldn't get any good results. So I gave up and started looking at other seminars. Maybe facebook ads and me don't mix. The learning curve with anything on the internet is quite long so get used to it. There are very few overnight success stories.

Brick And Mortar Businesses

The internet is only one part of the equation. Look around where you live and see how you can help the people in your area. All the easy to think about jobs are already gone. Like mowing lawns and cleaning up garages and backyards. One guy set himself up as the handy man and helped the people in his immediate area, for a price of course. It just brought in a bit of extra income.

To upgrade you need to start helping businesses make more money and that usually means helping them to get more clients or more customers. In a rather upmarket suburb of a big city, there was this alternative health clinic and it needed help. They were good at their job, but marketing was not one of their specialities. So I asked them what percentage they would give me for every paying customer I brought in. They were already offering a free session as a way to get people interested. So I wrote up a small introduction on an A4 size paper and just handed them out at lunch time. And the free offer got people in the door. Then I had to upgrade what they said to the clients, so they would come back.

I wanted a percentage of everything my clients spent in the clinic, because there was a lot of recurring business. You do not make very much money on the first visit. It is when they come back that is when you profit. So in my case of just getting a one off payment, while they could keep the client for many sessions was not in my best interest. Anyway, they soon realized if I went to another health clinic they could lose a lot of customers. So I got a percentage.

When I am discussing the idea to start promoting their business, I go for a percentage of everyone I bring in. A lot of businesses will realize the potential of having a freelance sales rep working on commission, because it doesn't cost them anything. And if it is a local business in your area, you can keep an eye on what is happening.

In any business you must keep contact details, like address, phone and email. So you can keep contacting them, even if it is only a letter or you hand deliver a leaflet to their physical mailbox. You must do this to survive. Just remember the money is in the list. Also this is your insurance. If you have any problems, you can take the list to a competitor and start selling the new business to your list. Or you can sell a similar product to your list from another business that is in the same niche.

Just remember, if you are good they are not going to let you go. And you get paid after they make money so they are happy. But you have to know what you are doing, so learn up on small business marketing and do your thing. As one marketer said "If you do 5% of what I tell you, you know more that 90% of the business owners out there." And small businesses need all the help they can get, especially in this economic climate.

Also if you are computer savvy you can help local business get on the internet. Set up a facebook page or a free website or a blog like Wordpress. Check Kindle for a 'how to book' and away you go. Say for $20 a week you will look after it.

At one stage I was offered a job selling websites but they were just rip-offs. I couldn't do it as I have to live in this town. I seriously considered setting up a little side business myself doing internet stuff. I still might there is definitely a need in this town.

Look around and see what your little corner of the city needs, then up-skill yourself on kindle and away you go. With the cost of entry being so cheap and you only need to learn one skill at a time. Now is the time to start a new business.

Teach English Online

The internet is new so money making ideas on the internet keep popping up regularly. These are new ways of making money that were not available a few years ago. One that hasn't really caught on, but is out there is teaching English online. Usually you have to match your time with Asia, South America and the Eastern Bloc countries as well as the Middle East. So if any of these time zones suit you, check it out.

Basically you need to find an agent in your target country where your time zones match up. And they either use skype or their own Learning Management System. The agent will have their own system in place and you just plug into it. To have a practice run teaching English online, go to italki.com and try and get a language partner in a country with a compatible time zone. Get as many language partners as you can and see if you like what you do.

With language partners get some in the country you want to teach online to. This way you can line up the time zone and see if it suits you. What I have found with language partners is a lot of people want to be language partners, but to actually get someone to talk to can be quite difficult. I keep sending messages on skype and if they don't answer or reply, I go to the next one on the list. The best language partners I have found are students as they have more free time. Get language partners in the best time zone that suits you, and teach to that country. If the time zones do not match up very well, you will not last as an online teacher.

Most people are very accommodating because they want to practice their English, as opposed to teaching their language. Just be careful, there are a few perverts out their. I have heard of people on other language partner sites having problems. Any problems just block them, and do the same on skype or qq or whatever video conferencing platform you use, like google talk or the yahoo one or the latest in Asia, Wechat. Most people are just happy to find somebody to talk too.

The only problem I've had with language partners, is actually finding someone to talk to. Maybe it is me but on skype I have a list of language partners and not many are on green. It takes a while to meet people on italki who will talk to you. I've found university students are the best as they are into learning. You actually might have to teach them how to teach on skype. What I usually do, is type in the chat box the sentence I am learning, and the student types in the translation in the language you are learning. I use two talkers, not at the same time, and type the same sentence to both to see if the answer is similar. Language is pretty flexible.

Also on italki you can become an online teacher and get students this way. Then you can put that down on CV when applying for a job. Also check out videos on YouTube about teaching, and you'll learn a lot about how to do things when teaching English. Most agents have a list of what you need to have when you apply. Bend the rules a bit when you are applying, just get the demo class. Then they will decide if they want you or more likely if they have enough students to keep you busy.

Google 'teaching English online' and see what pops up, and see if there is a book on kindle. Google is one of the best libraries on the planet, and it is at your fingertips, so check it out and see what you can find. Check out what you need to have to apply for the jobs. Then if you are really interested do a MOOC or two to put on your CV. A lot of companies are trying to sell an online course or a physical TEFL course, but do you really need one. You have to look at the cost of entry verses the return.

Language partners on Italki are free and that will give you real life experience. As opposed to book learning, and remember kindle is a lot cheaper than doing a course. To find a job you can also go through an ESL job site like ESLcafe.com and TEFL.com and see how many companies are looking for teachers. If you are already a teacher or a teacher aid you are ready to go. Check it out. I do recommend italki just to see if you like what you are doing, and to see if you are technically competent.

Set Yourself Up As A FreeLancer

If you do not want to go through an agent, check out the freelancer sites like guru, fiverr and upwork and become a freelance teacher. First check out how many jobs there are available and then go and get one. You can do your profile to suit the job, and then it is up to you to apply for the jobs and see what happens. Here you are not relying on anybody to get you a job you are doing your own thing.

I would not mention language partners on italki, because then your students could go to italki and get you for free. This way you can get one paying student and if you like it' get more. Now you are independent and that is the way to be. One thing to be aware of on the freelancer job sites is: they are also home to cheap companies looking for very cheap workers. So be careful.

The money is in the developed countries, like Saudi Arabia and other Middle Eastern countries as well as Japan and China. Check it out and see what you can come up. The first thing you must do is check the times. I use this website, 24timezones.com, they are very good. They even have a little clock you can download. Don't forget if you like talking to language partners register to become a teacher. At the moment there are too many English teachers on italki.

Better still if you find you like teaching, set yourself up on the freelancer sites.

To set yourself up as a freelancer with multiply skills, you will need to set up different accounts at different sites. Now Upwork.com is probably the largest but it is quite difficult to be accepted on the site. You can either set up one site, or set up three different skills on three different sites. I'd set up one site first and see what happens.

Just remember there is a learning curve. And when you have mastered the learning curve, you will be in a better position to set up a new site. On Guru.com you can set up multiply services under one name. So if you have more than one marketable skill set up another services page. They all have a free basic set up and above that you have to pay so much a month. It is up to you if you want to pay or not, but I would look at the return on investment first.

If you are helping people make more money, and you are good at what you do, then you should be able to start making money yourself. After that you could pay for extra. Also you should treat it like a job, and that means getting into the forum and uploading articles on their site to give you more exposure. Also you need to apply for jobs and that means putting in a quote, and describing how you will tackle the problem. It is not always about money. If you can somehow show them that you know what you are doing, then you might get the job. It is not always about money. I got one job mainly because the company was sick and tired of picking the cheapest and not getting the job done.

Selling Stuff

Another internet based idea that has gained in popularity, and is increasing more difficult to make extra money on, is eBay related auction sites. In the beginning it was easier to sell what you don't want, over the internet on the auction sites. But now the auction sites are dominated by companies, so it can be daunting just to try to be seen on these sites. But give it a go by all means and see what you can do. I have had very limited success on these sites, but with speciality items I have had some success.

When I closed down my bike fixing business I had lots of speciality tools, and I got a good price on the auction sites just selling them off separately. To be honest I would never have got that price anywhere else. The only other time we had some success, was when we brought another house and did some renovations. We sold the doors and windows easy. But with everything else I have had very limited success.

This leads over to rummage or garage sales. Here you are just getting rid of stuff you don't want, cheap. If it is not cheap people won't buy it. The people who go to rummage sales are looking for something cheap, so don't expect to make a ton of money doing this. This carries over to the weekend flea markets and their car boot sales. Where you take a load of stuff you don't want and try and sell it, with a lot of other people doing the same thing. Also here it is just luck that someone wants what you have at a price they are willing to pay. Quite entertaining but sometimes you end up buying too much. One guy I knew got a job in another city, and he sold up everything he didn't want just to get some money to buy gas and help him move. He did very well and he had years of accumulated stuff he wanted to downsize. He was lucky there were a number of second hand dealers in the market that day and he sold a lot of stuff to them.

When we were doing it, it was just a hobby, something to do on the weekends. If we made enough for a hamburger afterwards we were happy. In the markets the people who do well, usually have a little side business where they make their own stuff. The handmade soap sellers, jewellery makers, and the wooden toy maker all did reasonable well. They had a speciality product and they did all the markets, like the Saturday market and the night market as well as any other market they could find. And they sold over the internet. That was their side business. It gave them something to do and they loved doing it. All we were doing was selling excess stuff that we had accumulated over the years. And there wasn't much money in that. But it is a good day out.

We made a bunch of soap and tried that, but we must have done something wrong, as we didn't do too well. I think to survive in these markets you need to plan for the long term and market accordingly. That means collect email and physical addresses and follow up with letters and or emails. For this type of business, letters are probably better as you started off face to face and they know who you are. Just meeting people at the markets is not going to get you anywhere, you need to get contact details and follow up. The money is in the list. Markets are for meeting people and getting contacts then sell to your list. This is basic selling 101, but how many people do it. At the markets I would suggest it, but very few would actually do it. Because you usually always have to give something away for free. We used to give quarter blocks of soap away free. We had to make sure they knew it was soap, so they wouldn't feed the kids. For this we would get their physical address, and then start sending out letters. When you are selling something that is not very expensive it doesn't take very long before you hit break even with postage, so we used to sell packets of 5 or 10 to try and up the price. You must sell information you can't just sell your product. People like information, they don't like advertisements.

Now there is this site on the internet called etsy.com, where you can sell your home-made stuff and antiques. You need a credit card to join this site, but it is cheap to put products online. Like always you are up against the big players but if you are into making your own stuff, carve out a niche. With all auction sites, you have to go through the site and they guard their emails, so you can't sell off the site. You can only get the email after you have sold to your new customer. Now if you have a speciality item keep sending emails to your old customers. This way you do not need to go through the auction site and a customer who has brought once might buy again. Especially soap or jewellery or any product they use regularly. Etsy is another site to try out if you make your own stuff. When trading online you must get the word out, and that usually means where ever you can. So you should put your products up online where ever you can. The more places your products are online, the more chances you have of getting a sale. Etsy also has ebooks, and a lot of sites don't like ebooks, but then again Amazon and [Smashwords](#) have the market for ebooks.

As we are getting older now it was time to downsize. The kids had all left home and they dropped in occasionally with the grandkids and left a whole bunch of stuff behind that they would never need again. So we got on the auction sites and started selling off the excess and everything the kids left behind. Even here there is a learning curve and after some time we were pretty good at selling off the excess. Then we made the mistake of buying used furniture and other things people didn't want and tried to on sell them. And we ended up with a house fill of stuff we were trying to sell. Then we filled up my sister's house and now we can't move in both houses. So the moral of the story is just sell off your own stuff and not try to turn it into a business like we did. It was a lot of fun but we couldn't move in our house. Even now I don't know if we made any real money, we just used it as a tax right off.

Grow Your Own Vegetables

When you are living cheap in an uncheap world, saving money is as good as making money. Now everybody should have a vegetable garden. If you own your home turn your backyard lawn into a vegetable garden. Here you should check out websites for your area, so you can plant the right seeds at the right time. Gardening is like anything else. There is a learning curve and here you are learning by doing. So do it.

There are many books out there. Have a read and see what you would like to do. I follow the natural farming method out of Japan. That might look like the lazy man's way of gardening but it is not. If you want vegetables to eat you must look after the plants. My golden rule is not to plant too many seeds at the same time. I set up a nice sunny piece of lawn in the back garden and started with two square meters. Plants need sun, soil and water and they will grow themselves. So you don't need to go overboard, but you can for better results, if you want to.

Now if you live in an apartment or a flat and have no grass then it is time to get creative. I asked around the old retired people living in my street if they wanted a garden. I go to church so I asked around at the church and people are very helpful. The rules were quite simple. I'd grow it and they could eat want they wanted and I'd get the rest. And I had to look after the garden. I started off with one meter by two meters and the patch got bigger. I would only plant so many seeds each week and that way come harvest there were always plants growing.

I had to set up a net to stop the bugs, but that had to be done and was quite easy. I picked up some bamboo and bent them over like a tunnel and put insect cloth over them and that way we defeated the bugs. I had three gardens in three different addresses and we had to put the netting up over all the gardens. That was why they were only one meter wide. So I could cover them. Where I lived there were some pretty evil bugs that would eat everything. So we had to cover the vegetables. We also wanted to get some hedgehogs, but they are very hard to come by nowadays. I'm still after some hedgehogs to stop the slugs and snails. When I was growing up we had hedgehogs living in the garden. But now with roads and cars and dogs and cats, hedgehogs don't stand a chance.

Growing vegetables is a must for living cheap. Then learn how to blanch and freeze the excess. To live cheap you do need a freezer. A freezer is a must. We got ours from a rummage sale and it was cheap. At our local supermarket, when the meat gets close to its use by date, they drop the price to nearly half in a lot of cases. So we just buy the cheap meat and throw it in the freezer. We always have meat. We also buy the cheaper cuts of meat like pig feet and bones that we make into soup. But it is easier to buy cheap food at the supermarket that eat it so we ended up with a very full freezer. We had to revamp our buying habits.

Also we joined our local community garden and that was good. We helped out and we could get as much free vegetables as we could eat, and a lot of that ended up in the freezer. There are places where you can get free stuff in exchange for your time. Volunteering does pay off and in the long run you do come out on top.

Take Advantage Of High Prices

If you live in a country that demonizes cigarettes, and you have a bit of lawn in your back garden, put it in tobacco plants. And if you can make half way decent tobacco, then you are in business. But you have to check out the rules. When you are up against mega corporations and the tax department, you are bound to run into some pretty archaic regulations. In one OECD country it is legal to grow tobacco and make cigarettes, but you cannot sell home grown tobacco for cash, you have to trade it for something of equal value or something like that.

If you are going to get into this type of barter crop, you need to surround yourself with smokers. My mechanic smokes so he gets paid in tobacco, that kind of thing. Actually this type of barter crop hasn't really taken off, because turning tobacco leaves into something you can smoke is not easy. And that is where you have the advantage. Because a lot of people do not want to put up with the hassle of making tobacco. You could have the market to yourself. You would need to first check out what you need to do to make smokeable tobacco, then decide if the effort is going to be worth it. Google it and see what comes up. Check out the forums and see how active they are and join in. I will tell you now, the easy part is growing the plants and when the leaves are big enough, that's when the fun starts. You need to read up on how to make good tobacco and that is where Kindle comes in.

Another side venture you can look at, is home brew, that is making your own booze. Again, you have to look up how to make it and the cost involved. Same again get on google and check out the forums. Usually you end up making your own booze because you have grown too much fruit or potatoes, and you don't know what to do with them. It is not really difficult to make home brew, you just follow the recipe and away you go. Here again you are up against regulations, so see what you are allowed to do with the finished product. We have a couple of grape vines crawling along the fence, so we make a few batches of wine, to get rid of the excess. This is where going to the weekend flea markets as a seller has it's advantages. We just sell the excess, but even there you are up against regulations. If you have too much get a slot at the farmer's market and see what you can sell. We used to grow heaps of chard, because it is easy to grow and the bugs don't like it. But because it was so easy to grow nobody wanted it so we basically gave it away. We tried to sell it at the market so we could buy other vegetables that we didn't grow, but it was not very successful.

Another saving money venture that turned into a money making venture was firewood. We used to go to the beach, as we lived about 20 miles from the coast, and collect driftwood for the fireplace in winter. Because there was plenty of driftwood we ended up with heaps. We didn't have a chainsaw or any labor saving device, just a bow saw and a rip saw and a lot of energy. It started off as a winter day at the beach. People were fishing so we set a few fishing lines, then started collecting the wood. We cut the driftwood into lengths, so we could get it in the station wagon and trailer. This took a while and I dreamed of getting a chainsaw, but we got it done. Then when it was all loaded up we checked the fishing lines and usually didn't catch anything. Then headed home.

At home we got out the skill saw and cut it smaller so it would fit in the fireplace. Also on the way home we stopped off at the farm, and brought milk straight from the cow. Best milk I ever tried and cheaper than the supermarket. It was a good day out. So we were set for winter. But during winter we needed a bit of extra money, so I stuck a sign out the front of the house, and we were in business. It didn't take long before we were out of firewood, so it was back to the beach. That kept us going through the winter, and we made a bit of extra cash on the side. If you can think of places where you can collect firewood for free, like a forest or a patch of bush, then you are in business. If you see an old dead tree in someone's backyard, just ask.

Ask Around Generation

Another part of living cheap is the ask around generation. That is if you want anything, just ask. My computer crashed big time. Now I know a fair bit about computers, and people ask me to have a look at their computers if something is wrong. So I'm pretty clued up to do with tech. But this time I needed help so I asked everybody I knew. And within a few days I had it all fixed. And it all it cost was a couple of packets of biscuits. This is very basic networking. In business the gurus talk about networking, and here it is basically the same except on a lower scale. So you must meet people. I go to two different churches, an upmarket church and a down market church, and there I meet lots of people. It boils down to having a chat with people. At the flea markets I talk to the other stall holders. In the library I talk to other people. I also go to self defence classes at $5 a time and that is cheap. So I get around and I am always building my network.

Probably the best way to build your network is volunteering, and there are some very unusual volunteering opportunities out there. The best one I had was volunteering at a country radio station. There I get a chance to do a radio show over the air, but the benefits were the people. There I met experts in tech and many other skills that came in handy. One of volunteers had goats, and if she had too much milk she gave it away. She also had a big walnut tree. I would help out and get paid in walnuts and milk, as well as computer parts and computer knowledge.

Look around, ask around and see what is available. Check out the notice boards in cafes and supermarkets. And don't be afraid to ask. I wanted some bamboo for the garden and one guy had a bamboo hedge he wanted trimmed. I got the bamboo and he got his bamboo hedge trimmed. That's how it works. Volunteering is all about the people you meet.

Shopping

Now onto shopping. I've turned shopping into an art form. Anything that comes in the mailbox, I read. They are usually the specials and that is what you are after. I have alerts on all the supermarkets and department stores, so if any specials pop up I know about it. The weekly mailer from the supermarket is a must read. We have set prices, where we will only buy when the product meets that price. And you can get good deals doing this. But it also means you cannot have a fixed list of things you buy. We only buy what is on special. So what we eat is what is on special.

We have stopped eating bread and butter, as that was a major expense. And to stop eating bread, which is very difficult as we eat it all the time, was to increase the time before we brought more bread. So if we ran out we would wait a day or two before buying it again. And over time the distance between buying bread got longer and longer, so now we only buy good quality bread on special, which is not very often. Also as mentioned before we only buy meat and yoghurt that has been marked down, as it nears its use-by-date. Doing this you can get them around the half price mark. I usually buy vegetables at the flea markets, as they can be a lot cheaper than at the supermarkets. Also if we have too many vegetables that don't freeze very well, we sell them at the market and buy what we want. We grow vegetables to sell, so we can buy other vegetables.

One of my friends loved bread so much he wasn't going to give it up, even though it is a ridiculous price. So he brought an electric bread maker at a rummage sale for about $20 and never looked back. Now every time I go over for a visit he shows off his latest loaf. And I mean it is good bread, for under 50 cents he was saying. To live cheap you have to do it yourself and he did it himself.

When I read the newspaper I mainly read advertisements. When I see something like 40% off, that is when I look a bit closer. If I need to buy something, then I first look on the ebay related auction sites. To see what the second hand price is, as well as what the new price is. Then I go from there. I am never in a rush to buy anything. I take my time and look around. I even check out the opportunity shops, but lately they are getting more and more expensive. If I can get 40% off something brand new that I need or want then I'll go for it.

Another way to get a complete range of anything you want is garage or rummage sales. Here you can pick up some really good stuff cheap, but because it is so cheap you end up with a house fill of stuff. Sometimes you can't help but buy things that are so cheap. Now we are quite lucky there are auction sites on the internet that cover your area so you can on sell it, but that can take time. Now there are facebook buy and sell groups near where you live, so you can have a go selling on facebook. I've had more success selling on the auction sites than on facebook.

The Ultimate Get Out Of Debt

The ultimate "How to save money" is to go and live in a country where it is cheap to live. And I will admit there are a lot of cheap countries to live in, scattered around the globe. In a lot of cases you need a 4 year degree to get a working visa, but there are lots of ways around that minor hassle. As soon as you leave the western world and head into the developing world, things start to get cheap and in some cases very cheap. If you smoke cigarettes and don't want to give up, then heading into Asia or Latin America is a must where cigarettes cost less than a dollar, where as in some developed countries like New Zealand they can cost over $40 a packet. All that does is increase child poverty and family violence.

Because of the One Child Policy in China their poverty levels have dropped dramatically, and their education levels have gone through the roof. But as China has modernized so the prices have gone up. Rents are high now but buses and the subway is still very reasonable. And cigarettes are very cheap, and people there still give up. The first time I went to China nearly everybody smoked, now in the big modern cities very few people smoke. So taxing cigarettes to help families live in poverty is not really the way to go.

To start looking at cheap countries to live in, go to the "English as a Second Language" websites to get a feel for what is out there. When you use eslcafe.com you get jobs from around the world. That just gives you an idea of which type of jobs there are in what country. Now the big international sites where all the international companies advertise, usually all want a degree except for countries like Russia and some Central and South America countries. But it gives you an idea of what is out there.

If you are heading into Thailand check this out. This school offers some sort of student visa that will keep you in the country for a long time. You have to pay so much a month, and that beats running borders, unless you like running borders of course. You can find it on http://eslcafe.com/ under the heading 'Get a Degree and End Debt Free" at this school http://siamtechnology international.com/ba-tesol.html I checked it out and it seems legit.

Now while you are getting into the swing of things, start looking at YouTube on teaching ESL. Youtube is the best teacher on the planet, so use it and learn. Watch videos and learn. Then check out the MOOCs, there are a few on Teaching ESL. This is one here https://www.futurelearn.com/courses/english-language-teaching. I've done this one, https://www.coursera.org /course/ shaping2paths, and the interaction on the forums will teach you more about teaching than any university course. So do it and then it looks good on your CV.

Next up pick a country and find out as much as you can. You need the website for the local jobs where the local companies advertise for teachers or other jobs. In China the website is echina cities.com. Here you will find out everything you need to know about China. If you want to go to China check it out this book on kindle, "Teach and Travel in China." This book is a brief introduction to living cheap in China. In Vietnam in Hanoi the site is tnhvietnam as well as a host of facebook pages. For Vietnam check out this book "Live and Teach in Vietnam." These local sites are the sites you are looking for, where the local companies advertise. To find these sites you need to do a lot of searching. You also need to look up the backpacker sites, so you can find a place to live. A lot of jobs actually have accommodation supplied, which is where I would start. One type of job I do not like, is when you go from school to school teaching a class here and a class there. A lot of travelling. In Japan they give you a car and in Vietnam you get a motorbike. Not my idea of a job.

The internet makes life very easy. Next get onto italki and find some language partners in the country you want to go to. Most just want to talk in English, and if you find one that will actually help you learn the language you are doing well. Here you are getting boots on the ground experience without actually going there. When you have decided on a country and a city, join the expat sites and join in the conversation. Make a few friends before you leave town. You never know you could get an apartment and a job from your living room.

If you are a bit worried about teaching English and living in a strange country, look at the volunteer opportunities and see if you can do that for a couple of months. Try and get one with free board and food. I've seen volunteer jobs advertised where you have to pay everything plus your time. If they can't offer board and food, then I usually look somewhere else. In saying that, there are some really good volunteer jobs out there. These give you a starting point. While you are there you can check out the job market and whatever, and be set up when your volunteer time is over. Dave's http://eslcafe.com/ has a number of volunteer positions advertised.

Now, do you need an ESL certificate or not? Yes you do need something, but just a few MOOCs should be enough. In Vietnam they always ask for an ESL Certificate so it is a good idea to get one. At a number of jobs I went for they didn't even look at my passport. In developing countries out of the big cities, foreigners are few and far between so you are in demand.

In a cheap country teaching English part time, life was very easy. I had no trouble paying the bills. But that all changed when I arrived back in civilization. Before I was saving money, now I was spending my savings.

In a cheap country, you have to put up with different things like toilets, everyday privacy, and pickpockets. But I think that is nothing compared to what you have to put up in the civilized world. I had more problems adapting back to the west, than I did adapting to a country where I didn't speak the language, and most often didn't know what was going on. This was before mobile technology became mainstream.

Now when you head overseas, life is easy as long as nobody pinches your mobile phone or tablet. The first thing you need to do is get an account at a mobile company, and anybody at a backpackers will help you do that. But even before you leave your home country you can load up with maps and Lonely Planet guidebooks and you are set. Hopefully everything you need is in the palm of your hand. But and this is a very big but, keep it safe, because there is a thief out there trying to get it. I used to carry money in all pockets and when you wear cargo pants you have lots of pockets. But then someone cut one of my pockets, so now I wear shirts with lots of pockets.

The Last Word

These are the ways I use to get out of debt and stay there and they work for me. Living frugally is a sort of mentality that I have instilled in my brain over the years. Now it is basically automatic. Sometimes it has its disadvantages as I seem to buy things I see marked down. Like the other day I was in the supermarket, and there was a packet of sausages at half price, so I brought them. More out of habit than anything else, cause there was hardly any room in the freezer. It has got to the stage where I will only buy things like food on special. It is quite simple, if it is not on special I wait till it is. I don't know if that is a good thing or a bad thing, but it suits me. At the moment that is the way I like to live and it suits me. Most people at the supermarket, know I only buy the marked down products. And that means shopping everyday and if nothing is cheap I just walk out.

I have the garden and my internet thing and that keeps me happy. So life is quite simple and that is the way I like it.

Now I work at the factory on minimum wage for 4 to 6 months then I head over to Hanoi, Vietnam for 6 months. There I live in a homestay where I teach English for an hour and a half a day on weekdays and in return I get free accommodation and dinner. The rest of the time I teach outside and get paid and usually make enough to cover the airfares and expenses. It is a good life and Hanoi is very cheap.

Make an Author Happy Today

If you found the material in this book helpful, I'd be eternally grateful if you took two minutes to write a review on Amazon. When you leave a review, it helps other teachers find my books.
https://www.amazon.com/dp/B08Q1RMZYX
Your review will make my day.

Thank you!

Peter LeGrove

Other Books By Peter LeGrove

Teach and Travel in China

Live And Teach In Vietnam

Reading Student Struggling Student

Teach English as a Second Language to Children

How To Add Qualifications To Your CV Using FREE Courses

How To Make An Online CV Using Free Software

Survive and Thrive on the Road to your Future

Survive and Thrive on the Road to your Child's Future

Get Out Of Debt

Is Vegetable Gardening For You

Live Cheap in an UnCheap World

Is Civilization Collapse Happening Now

Are you Ready for Civilization Collapse

How To Save Money

Thank you and all the best on you excursion into the get out of debt world. I hope you have a wonderful time like I did.

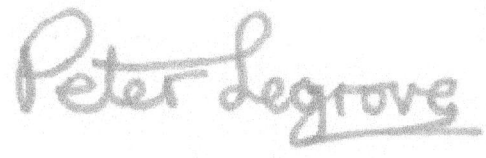

Peter Legrove

plegrove@gmail.com

www.animalsdinosaursandbugs.com

Live Cheap In An UnCheap World

Disclaimer: Although the author and publisher have made every effort to ensure that the information in this book was correct at press time, the author and publisher do not assume and hereby disclaim any liability to any party for any loss, damage, or disruption caused by errors or omissions, whether such errors or omissions result from negligence, accident, or any other cause.

This book is for entertainment purposes only. The views expressed are of the author alone and should not be taken as expert advice. The reader is responsible for his own actions. Neither the author or the publisher assume any liability or responsibility on behalf of the reader or purchaser of this material.